Jessie the Galaxy

Based on the true story

Gem Hutchens

Jessie the Galaxy
Copyright © 2020 by Gem Hutchens

All rights reserved. No part of this publication may be reproduced, distributed, or transmitted in any form or by any means, including photocopying, recording, or other electronic or mechanical methods, without the prior written permission of the author, except in the case of brief quotations embodied in critical reviews and certain other non-commercial uses permitted by copyright law.

Tellwell Talent
www.tellwell.ca

ISBN
978-0-2288-2169-4 (Paperback)
978-0-2288-2170-0 (eBook)

For my daughter Ada, who lights up my life

Part One

Chapter 1

The Isolation Room

That was the day I went crazy. I held my eighteen-month-old daughter, dialled 911, and asked them to come to arrest my husband or I would jump off the roof with little Aisa in my arms. I felt the guilt like a lead block on my chest because I imagined that my husband had murdered his family, and I wanted him in jail right away. I did tell him I had been jittery and wide-awake for a few nights and had not slept, but I didn't tell him that I called one of his friends at midnight.

The phone in my hand droned for years in the darkness.

"Why are you still here?" I yelled at him with the blurred vision of the spectacle in my head.

Sitting in the dining room, my husband told me to call the number on the card. I had gone mad after hearing what he said. He was dreading the imprisonment that would result from a crime that I had insanely created in these sleepless nights. I couldn't tolerate the glare of the white business card on the table under the daylight with its little green and blue lines printed at the corner—a business card for a consultant from Coastal Health.

While I explained the situation to the 911 operator, my husband grabbed Aisa from my hands.

"You are insane!" he screamed and took her to the living room.

Shortly, two police cars arrived. The doorbell buzzed, and I ran downstairs to open the door. I didn't even look at the cops—the car door was opened.

Sitting in the back of the cruiser, I looked at the cop behind the wheel, her long black hair neatly wrapped into a lower bun on her neck. She eased the car away from the curb, the red and blue flashing lights chasing behind. These lights didn't look like colours from pigments flattened on the palette in the conventional sense. They were more like whitest white blazes chopping my hair. The police car was hushed, and the steering made me queasy—not that she was driving too fast, but my brain was involuntary wobbly.

"So, tell me what's wrong," said the police officer.

Sitting in the back of the police car, with a metal grid barring the small window, even though I knew nothing about the officer who was speaking to me, I thought that she was the only person in the world to whom I could tell the truth. I felt soothed, tipping my head to bulletproof violet window glass, and bounced back from the wave of heat under the solar radiation. I didn't want my hair to get static electricity.

"My husband killed my mother-in-law and sister-in-law. They were both on the ship when it flipped over. He did something to the boat and killed them all! Every single passenger on board! They all died!" I was strangely energized by what I had just said.

The police officer didn't respond; she continued to drive in silence.

I was thinking about him killing my father-in-law with poison too. But I was too tired to explain more, mainly because the police officer didn't seem to be listening to me. I wanted to nap in the car. I hadn't slept in a while.

Later, I followed her into a room. A man sat inside writing on pad of paper. I sat down with him. I watched him move his pen speedily across the page for four lines and realized that it was a doctor's note. I became angry.

I shook my head and forced a laugh. "How can you write so much? I haven't even said anything yet!"

The police officer looked at me but said nothing. I hoped that she had already observed that the doctor was a fraud. He stood up and spoke with the officer. He was a tall Indian man with a bit of silver hair at his temples. His gravelly voice made him sound like a very stern authority, so I was too scared to argue anymore. I looked into the police officer's keen eyes, which seemed to speak as they stood out against her smooth dark skin. I was nervous and uncertain regarding what the officer and the doctor would do, so I asked the police officer if I could speak with her privately.

"To tell you the truth," I said, "it's actually my fault. I'm having an affair with a man and cheating on my husband, you know? There is a man... well, he wanted to have sex with me."

I was thrilled to finally say it because I'd felt so ashamed that the man had been haunting me for the past few weeks.

Am I acting? I thought.

The police officer didn't respond to anything I said. She just left me alone, standing outside of the doctor's room. After a while, a nurse gave me a small clear container. She met my gaze with a pair of uninhabited, glacial blue eyes with small jet pupils as though I were her enemy—an eclipse eye contact kept in view. I went inside a bathroom and heard the water dripping down the pipe from the ceiling. Suddenly, two drilling sounds murmuring in the air, rattling the tissue and container on the sink.

The ear-shattering drilling rhythmically sounded gliding through the air.

"It's a trick!" James, the man who spoke with the Spanish accent, haunted me. *"They are going to analyze you! DON'T trust them."*

Vigorous thumping emanated from my heart. *What do I do with this?* I watched the small pellucid container as I peed in the toilet.

I could no longer hear him, even as I listened carefully and tried to talk to him. This made the voice seem even more real, so I really believed his existence. I was worried because it sounded as if he might have left.

I quickly filled up the container with tap water and put it on the nurse's counter. It was a sterile urine container.

I thought the nurses' working station would be equipped with advanced technology, such as Qubit, holographic displays, and ultra-sci-fi gadgets. It was the Neuron Era—an era where sound, transmitted through the skin into a human being's cranial nerves, propagated to link biometric identifiers such as fingerprints and retinal scans.

The fonts that I saw on the signs were refracted to other words. Richmond became San Diego (where James lived).

The advertising message on the billboard read: PEANUT BUTTER AND MILK ARE SOUL MATES. JELLY WAS JUST A FLING. But then transformed into Spanish fonts: MANTEQUILLA DE MANÍ Y LECHE SON ALMAS GEMELAS. JELLY FUE SÓLO UNA AVENTURA.

The forest in the world looked ridiculously gigantic, and the shiver of wind among the trees whispered to the leaves and branches, which rustled, fluttered, and shivered under the sunbeams. They were passing melodies by vibrating human skin, a kind of plainchant from the Middle Ages.

The trees looked the way they had at Stanley Park when I'd lost my temper and wanted my husband to turn back and go home. He'd driven us to Stanley Park, where the little train was, intending to ride with our daughter, but I had to leave. I heard the trees soulfully singing loudly with expression, but no one could hear what I heard, which drove me to madness.

I spotted the monitors sitting on the nurses' table. They looked so old that they tricked the naked eyes. Another dimension had hidden within these vintage shells. The nurses kept their shapes low-key and greyish blue and acted neutral and impervious. I caught their airwaves transmitted through the skin, but my nerves, played from heartstrings, were soon concealed because I had intruded their realm of propagation of voice.

"Hey," he said. *"I'm still here. You hear me?"* It was James—his voice in my head when I walked into a waiting room. A TV was on. At least I could still hear him.

"You are so beautiful," he said. *"I am watching you."* A news reporter behind the TV screen was watching me. My nerves were monitored behind the scene. This thought made me jump off the chair and leave the room. There was an unknown group of hackers observing and recording my every step.

"You almost made it!" James said. *"You are a genius! Finally! I am the God now. Thank God!"*

I walked out to the hallway and digested his meaning. He was the genius who was being monitored by the hackers, but he was free because I figured out the transmission and heard the voices so he could be on top of us. I became the genius who was monitored.

Does that mean he died though? I thought that my husband had killed him as well and that he now lived in another world and that—as he said—he was the God.

A bespectacled male nurse came to take me to a room. He looked like Jack Nicholson. He wanted me to take my shoes off and get on the bed.

Later a large, box-like machine with a hole in the centre appeared above my head and began spinning.

I went out and saw a row of people lying on pink beds. It seemed to be invisible to them—the box-like machine. They looked bored, tired, numb, and pain-free.

Where the hell is it?

The doctor called me to a cell. I saw a mattress against the left wall and a lidless silver toilet bowl at the right corner.

A PRISON? What did I do? I thought in shock and despair. I laughed at myself for having lost. Ironically, my husband had won. Evil had won. I hated him then.

So, this was it. This was my life. I was in jail because I'd had an affair. For the rest of my life, my husband would take care of our daughter as if nothing had happened.

I stopped at the door before the guard closed it. I didn't want to go inside.

"Do you want to say something?" the doctor asked.

"Can I make a phone call?"

The guard gave me my phone, and I called an Indian man who was a customer of my husband's company. Dal was his name. My job was translating in business, and he would call me occasionally and chat. The last time we had sat down had been in the office, and Dal had cleared his throat and straightened his crotch after our brief talk. We regarded each other as friends, and I hoped that he would help me get out of here. He didn't pick up the phone after it rang for ages.

He is probably dead, too.

The door closed. Several locks clicked into place. I was in a psychiatric isolation room for two days.

The doctor's certificate of diagnosis read:

> **This 29-year-old married mother of an 18-month-old daughter was admitted as a certified patient to the psychiatric Unit of Richmond Hospital. At the time of admission, the patient was intensely delusional, disoriented, psychotic, and preoccupied. It was difficult to have any proper communication and make connections. The patient was responding to messages, was hearing voices, and had the delusion of destroying her family, including her 18-month-old daughter.**

I looked up at the ceiling, where there were three rows of white fluorescent lamps in silver metal reflectors. Lying on the mattress, I found that I could see my reflection in the metal. James had hidden up there, peeking at me as he lay naked. All of a sudden, my heart began to pound hard.

"Here she comes," said James.

The soft clicking sound of a stapler chirped in my ears—made me listen carefully.

A loud crash sounded as someone committed suicide by throwing themself from the roof. I had heard it hundreds of times before bedtime at night. Death didn't like that James had taken my soul.

I shall be the one who dates him.

We'd met in a laundromat. The Death of the human body was in an Indian man's flesh, feral and gangly with dark skin. Under his dry, coarse, curly hair were his eyes, fierce and sharp, aimed at the target. My life was under his control.

The walls beside the bed had been scarred by desperate fingernails. Several ear-splitting suicide jumps happened continuously; it was not a pleasant rhythmic beat but dreadful punishment.

Meanwhile, a new voice emerged, seemingly from right outside the door: A baby's stroller bumped into the wall, as its wheels spun too fast for it to brake. It sounded familiar because it was the stroller that my husband and I used to carry our daughter in when we went out for walks.

Thinking that my husband had come to pick me up, I jumped off the mattress and looked through the small window in the door. But what I saw was a white wall on the other side. The loud, clanking crash of the stroller plagued me even more because my daughter was sitting inside it.

Are you stupid?

I was mad at my husband because he couldn't find a way to get me out and kept getting stuck in the same place.

I was an intersected signal receptor—like one of the Teletubbies. On the ceiling, I saw the reflection of the empty corner spot on my mattress. I wondered whether I could see James from a different angle if I moved a little bit more in this direction or that.

"Numb(er) code?" The nurse asked James impatiently since she already knew the answer.

"AN. (an Angel in Neuron)."

I heard James start arguing with the nurses outside, saying that the code was right. *Angel* was how people referred to themselves in Neuron. He was the *God* who instructed the Angels about the old-time era upstairs. Both of us exchanged the code of fingerprints and connected to our neurons so we could hear each other in our brains. James shared the cipher that existed between the nurse and himself so I could hear them. I was eager to listen to his lecture, and he also wanted me to be there!

"Fun, isn't it?" said James to me. *"We are the light racer."*

He was reading my mind. The blue-eyed nurse was kind of jealous that James liked me. She was the one taking my urine sample. She stared at me when I looked out the room window. The hostilities pulled my string like frostbite, decomposing my brain's grey matter, affecting mind and feelings. James had come to check on me through the window—myriad blinking milliseconds. I was so close to catching the shadow of his head several times because of his dizzying speed.

"James, I am not impatient!" said the nurse. "They are the patients... Hi, welcome back to Neuron again. See you in a bit."

The nurse seemed annoyed at having to take care of numb and monotonic in-patients in the topsy-turvy ward. James was busy lecturing to Angels newly descended while trying to negotiate with the nurse for my release.

"Are you patient?" James asked the nurse. *"Or are there too many paths for you to find empathy?"*

"No, I am impatient to shorten the paths for 'em paths of recovery," said the nurse promptly as reminded by God.

"Within inside or outside the physics?" said God.

"Inside," said the nurse.

"What is God?" said God.

"Go(d) who go(t) it," said the nurse.

"Solid," said the God. *"A voice listener?"*

"A genius," said the nurse.

"Spell, please," said God.

"Gene in us," said the nurse rolling her eyes.

"Thank you for reading."

Wham! James slammed the book with the force of a thousand suns. He didn't even bother to take a glance at the page—*The Angel Code of Ethics*, a book that he just got for his new job.

"UNLOCK AN, please," he said.

"There's a bug. Sorry, James," said the nurse assertively but with a heavy sigh.

"Fuck!" said James loudly, and whining echoed in the hallway. *"I'm missing an Angel in Neuron!"* His voice emerging distinctly sonorous and nasal.

He is trying hard to get me to the Angel! Now is the perfect time to punch the door and make him talk to me face to face!

"I'm missing ONE..." he continuously whined in the hallway.

I sprang out of bed and looked out the window on the door. Only a cloudy white wall covered up the right side. I tried to look all around the window very carefully. *Can I see James from a different angle?* I saw nothing and started to feel disappointed in myself.

"James, she is (be)spectacled," said the blue-eyed nurse.

No, I'm not watching your spectacle! I took my glasses off and smashed the frame and lenses with both hands. A sudden light smoky haze smell and the odour of burning metal or electronics breathing in the nose. I then went back into bed and crossed my legs in a meditation position.

"What is she doing?" asked the nurse, watching the screen monitor.

"She wants to die," said James.

"Interesting," said the nurse.

"Watch your words," James replied.

I stopped my breath to see if I could be dying in this way.

Those chirping clicking sounds returned, prepared for counting my breaths.

1, 2, 3... 32, 33, 34... 80, 81, 82, 83... 101, 102...

I breathed a little bit and tried again.

1, 2, 3… 32, 33, 34… 80, 81, 82, 83… 101, 102, 103… 201, 202, 203…

"Come on! You can do it!" said the nurse and came other nurses to watch.

1, 2, 3, 4, 5, 6, 7, 8, 9, 10, 11, 12, 13, 14, 15, 16… 78, 79, 80, 81… 101, 102, 103… 201, 202, 203… 320, 328, 339… 400, 405, 406…

I began counting the wrong numbers because of the lack of oxygen to my brain. All voices slowly fading away, my whole body became airy without consciousness. The flesh would atone for the people who committed suicide, plagued by mental distress. The thought of dying didn't martyr me. They expounded my existence, my entire degree of reliability seemed to throw off saying, "Hi!"

My head began drooping, along with my shrunken sitting body and bones, away from the wall. A warm current unconsciously slowly coursing through my bottom half, creating an increasing sense of well-being and relaxation—the feeling of death that I could imagine.

Then a rising urine smell, for I had peed the bed.

I didn't make it. I am still in this room. I'd like to die at once, rather than becoming demented and rotting here until death. Fuck off, God, Angel, or genius. Why am I here? Where are my daughter and husband? Why am I stuck in this room?

A nurse carrying a meal tray came in with two guards. "What's your name? Do you know where you are?" the nurse asked.

The questions she asked sounded stupid. Apparently, she knew the answers. Why bother me to say why I was there?

Just take me to the course.

From the other window over the top, I looked at the antenna perched on the red-brick building.

Are the guardsmen here to bring me up? Can I be an Angel now?

The cloudless sky looked hyper-real.

"How are you feeling?" asked the nurse. "Are you okay?"

I looked up, and the two blurry tall guardsmen who stood by me looked away. I felt that they had been sent from the Abyss and were judging me as they stared at my harmless appearance.

Can I be an Angel now?

The nurse handed one white and one blue pill in the white wrapper and waited while I swallowed them.

In the end, I fell asleep on the bed, my brain finally shutting down for a while. The pale, yellow twilights… dense darkness explained the nighttime… the spine-chilling moment of being alone. I felt protected by the sounds from the nurse working at the station outside. The stapler clicking sounds and all the strange voices were gone in the air for a rest.

I woke covered with a blanket, curled up at the corner of the mattress. I went to touch the side of the bed where I peed. It was still wet.

What the hell am I doing here?

My head was drowned and dizzy like I hadn't slept for years, but that little nap kindled the dying embers.

Above the ceiling, the sound of water racing down a pipe, a chair scratching the floor, bumping off the furniture, the course had taken so long. No, it was Death and unknown ghosts debating in the colosseum-like plaza. I must be in the Abyss now, hearing the verdict, the voices not letting me go.

I failed in my commitment to die for them.

The image of the demons was haunting me like the black spirits that swooped down on me when I opened the door. The way to the house upstairs was through the dark garage where my husband put the dead body of Gucci—our white and light brown papillon—in a black garbage bag for a couple of days. She died in a car accident. I went back home after burying her corpse beneath the dirt of Davis riverbank with my husband and daughter. That happened in the blink of an eye when the black spirits jumped into my vision. I heard the claws grounding the concrete floor with a flock of shadowy wings dashing to me. They passed through me and fled outside of the door when I opened it.

I saw Gucci.

Waking up in the morning, my death was just a sleep from the pill. I must have been scorned by people. The air had a moment of quiet until I saw the door being opened by the daylight. I thought I was blind when the light shot in through the door.

Chapter 2

Transmission

I felt that I was clutched onto something due to the blindness and immobility of being without my glasses. I closed my eyes when I sat into an "exorbitant shift," which would be transmitting me upstairs to see James. My eyelids were fitfully swept with lights and shadows like riding on the carousel. It was a cracking tunnel that bypassed the time tunnel. I couldn't wait to see the absolute beauties, playfully quirky novelties or creatures that I couldn't describe. I could have just passed the Earth and the Abyss now because I heard human voices talking. To minimize the interruptions, I didn't want to glance in case I was caught by the ghost and lost the chance to see James. I felt the direction in the circle was changed.

A roar like an engine revving up along a straight line, accelerating within a second. Then all the bad, shameful, evil things were gone. I thought I was in Neuron because of the dizzying speed.

I could be dead already.

I opened my eyes and saw my mother-in-law and sister-in-law. If they were alive, then what about those imaginations? Did I save them? They looked like they lost part of their memories—I *remembered* how they died. Were the memories erase by the exorbitant shift? I was about to ask if they knew the truth of their shipwreck. My mother-in-law approached me with a warm smile. She held up my right hand, and I took it.

"Mom," I said, "your hand is so cold. How are you?"

"I am fine," she said with eyes full of sympathy.

My sister-in-law leaned in to hug me. "Oh my God, I've missed you!"

I felt innocent of what she said. I'd missed them as well.

Our family friend Yumi came in with a bouquet of yellow daisies. It seemed like everyone was alive. It took me a while to adapt to the emptiness without hearing weird voices. Broadening surrounded me with thick dark blue curtains.

Am I on the same floor as James now?

After they left, I jumped off the bed. I peeked into a room with a big glass window and saw two blue-uniformed women. They seemed to be working in the control tower at the airport, looking at their logs and monitors whenever an airplane landed. I'd been in the first bed near them.

I felt cold. I approached one of the women.

"Can I take a shower, please?"

Being an Angel, you have to be friendly, clean, and smell good. A nurse gave me some clothes and toiletries and then showed me where the bathroom was.

It was a spacious bathroom with a yellow brick floor. There was a toilet with a rail, a sink and a mirror, and a showerhead. I was disappointed to be in just another hospice for the elderly because of setting. I wasn't dead after all. I took off my striped black and white sweater and the dirty black pants I had worn for many days.

While I was taking a shower, I was surprised to discover my anus was back to normal. Before, it had a lump caused by the pregnancy. Now it was totally healed. I was so happy that my anus was not swollen anymore because my body had gone through the exorbitant shift that can cure all the pains and wounds.

Am I back to my teenage body?

After my sweet shower, I put on a brown gown, for I was certified as an Angel, and I kind of liked this uniform. It felt refreshing to walk around and explore the environment. The big French window in the middle flashed into view two-sided covering with four mountainous, dull-blue curtains without any solid doors or walls. There seemed an aircraft collided head-on in front of the window.

It was a titanic, airy, and isolated asylum.

The light had been filtered, and the sound had been proofed—the air was vacuumed, just like people's minds. I felt like walking in the smoggy clouds when the shimmering halo illuminated the white vinyl floor as if enveloped in the germless stardust.

A fragile silver-haired old woman was eating peacefully by herself in the centre of the hall. She was small and quiet. When I sat down in front of her, I felt as though I were looking at a mirror.

"Would you like something to eat as well?" asked the nurse.

I looked up and nodded to the nurse.

The old woman stared at me, and I stared back. She kept her eyes on me in a cold implacable manner; it was uncomfortable. Disagreeable. But she looked just like me, only her eyes weren't brown but tea green. She also had a relatively long gap between her nose and upper lip—thin and firm. She had a tiny jaw and flimsy cheeks that were shrunken and wrinkled.

Is this me after forty years?

My mother had a dream of a British family from England who told her that she was a British in her past life—a paranoid thought from a Chinese teaching English—but I thought of my mother when I looked at this old lady.

The nurse brought a meal tray, but I was only interested in the yogurt.

"What brought you here?" I asked her.

She stared at me and didn't say anything. It was an awkward question that produced nothing but an awkward moment between us.

My husband came to see me, but I didn't want to talk to him yet.

After he left, I went to ride an exercise bike. I watched the red digits increasing on the small monitor and thought it was a trigger and that, if I could pedal rapidly enough, the world will be flipped. But nothing happened although the digits kept adding up with my pedalling.

It's just because I am too weak.

After fiddling with the bike, I found a corner area with a TV hanging from the ceiling. I sat down and craned my neck to watch a soccer game. I thought of my daughter.

What is she doing right now?

James was the doctor-on-call and would come to check me later at night. This thought brought me fulfillment.

The room was cold even with the heavy quilt cover. I lay down on the bed, expecting Dr. James would come to check until I woke up in the middle of the night. There was one time I missed when somebody lifted the curtain, and my brain couldn't help thinking about the check-up. Finally, I caught a torchlight shined to my bed, and I squinted very carefully. That was just the nurse.

What if James is the patient on the next bed?

The small empty gap between the curtain and the floor and the occasional rustling noise behind it were very suspicious. I wanted to jump off and lift the curtain, but I hesitated.

The world had flipped that day when I was done showering and came out from the shower room. I felt someone was watching me naked somewhere in the bathroom, and the lights were flickering in the mirror and looked bizarre. James was in the mirror, watching me. I quickly grabbed my towel and felt my heart pounding very fast. I didn't realize where that impulse came from, but it just happened without any clue. I did sometimes browse old friends' Facebook, so I didn't make him unique. Until I lay down here, thinking about who he was. Back when I was dating in 2009, I wondered why this man appeared in my mind, unexpectedly.

That day, James was late to the film class. He came only four to five times that semester, just like a visitor. I came out from the darkroom having finished loading the 16 mm film onto the reel. I was doing the developing process, so I had to pay attention to the clock hung on the wall every five to six minutes. While I was processing the films, I headed up and saw he was standing under the clock and watching me jiggling the knob. He gave me a slight smile.

"Hey!" I said. "How long have you stood there watching me?"

I blushed and couldn't concentrate on the work anymore. I looked down my shirt's neckline to make sure it was not too low. While we all were waiting for the bleaching time, the professor called him to tidy up the dry films in the human-height storage rack. I passed by him and saw he was miserably untangling the little shrunk films with his fingers. I would've stopped and asked him if he needed help, but I didn't. I didn't want to interrupt his upset. It was a chance to talk to him, but I missed it.

I started noticing his lanky figure. He always wore a black beret and hung around with a shorter friend who was more plump with long curly black hair tucked in a green cap. James came to class the week after and took part in a critique—a session where art students showcase their works and have them discussed by their peers. There was only me in the class that day presenting the film. I was influenced by Maya Deren when I studied film at grad school in Boston. So the assignment I showed in the class that day was a black and white, eccentric, meaningless bit of experimental cinema. That was just a practice of life. The only thing that could be mentioned was a dead rat. I got a close-up shot of the corpse above with a few flies hovering on the street.

I sat at the front of the screen and signalled the professor in the control room to wind my film. When the light from the film projector was shone into the room, James came. It became like my debut. Film was a declining subject, so there were only four to five students in the class. And there were four that day, including James. The room was still very empty, and he could've just sat behind, but I felt the chair behind me quietly being moved. The sole of my left foot cramped like a chicken claw. Hearing only the whirring sound from the film projector behind. I leaned back to let him see more of the screen. The air had gone silent with the last chopping and stripping images.

"Any thoughts, comment about Jessie's film?" the professor said and turned the lights dim.

James initiated the talk. He poured out words with confidence and composure to the professor. I felt sheltered by his broad shoulders within the grey sweater. I also felt at a loss. I avoided his eyes several times—otherwise, I would fall into a starry night or a wormhole. I couldn't remember what he said.

"Weird things in life," I said at one point so quietly that the professor didn't even hear.

James didn't agree with me. He was positive about that silly film I made, and that was the only comment I got that day. That was the only time I talked with him in real life—and the second missed opportunity to speak more with him.

I'd been quite interested in his existence ever since. But I did have a "sort of" boyfriend in a long-distance relationship at the time. I saw James in different places, like working in the welding studio. And one day, I saw him lying on the couch reading by himself in the library. The books I wanted were located in the last couple of rows on the shelves at the corner where he sat.

It was a rainy day. I grabbed another book to read until I worked up the nerve to go to the shelf at the back, but by then he was gone. That was the third missed opportunity.

The very last time I saw him was on my way from the main building to Mission Hill studio. It had been a long time since he'd seen me in film class. I saw he was still wearing his black beret as he walked down the hill with his friends. I walked uphill alone and noticed him coming towards me. I looked aside from the traffic island in the middle of the roads. It would be bizarre if I decided to jaywalk—we were doomed to bump into each on the street without any way to escape today.

I had to pull up my socks as we had not seen each other for a while. I saw he was talking to his friends and watching me in the distance. It was so sunny that day, I put my head up and gave him a huge smile when he approached.

I regretted it right away. That smile was too big, like thousands of words coming out at once. I probably looked a little crazy even though he smiled back at me.

Within a couple of months—just before I graduated—I saw that his artwork won first place in the school's painting contest. I looked carefully at his painting: a car painted in white on a serape. I purposely passed by the welding studio and checked the corner in the library. I sat on the beanbag where he sat before and stared out the raindrops rolling down the window glass. We were not classmates anymore.

We would be strangers ever after.

I had to pay something for failing to embrace the opportunities God had offered. I had confidence that he wouldn't reject an Asian girl if I took the initiative. I would have a profound relationship that ended up a painful break-up, but I intentionally avoided it. I was too lucky to earn the perfect life I had right now even though the consequence would be the same with or without the relationship with James. I had been so smart to shorten the path to be successful. Thus God waited until I had a lovely husband and healthy daughter and then penalized me with mental illness, without superficial trauma but the ridiculous malingering. Therefore, these image fragments of James seemed to make sense now.

The preoccupied thoughts didn't stop me. I decided to check the next bed. At night, I held my breath and lifted up the curtain to have a quick look. I saw a young Asian boy lying on the bed on his back. I jumped back to my bed and closed my eyes.

I'd spent two days in intensive care, in the morning, the nurse sent me to another department.

The "transmitter" was the same one who sent me from the isolation room to the intensive care. She was a Caucasian in her fifties with short curly hair, a chubby robotic-looking woman in glasses. She was blue-eyed, the same era group as the nurse, the same coldness—with a facial expression that seemed to say, *"Somehow you made it."*

On the way to another floor, I realized that the exorbitant shift I imaged was just a wheelchair. The lifting sound that I had perceived as a dazzling time tunnel was an elevator. The nurse moved me so quickly that the scenes jumped into my eyes as a series of impressionist paintings. A middle-aged blond woman with a floral dress opened her mouth and laughed out loud while sitting in the wheelchair and talked to a man who stood in front of the piano playing jazz. Some crayons were scattered on the table and floor; a group of youths had just finished and run away. There were rich hues of light and an atmosphere that looked so old.

Time had worn.

I arrived at the bed again. I'd been trying hard to fall asleep for a while. My brain kept busy running thoughts that never stopped for a break. They were as stubborn as my firm will that was observing them.

"Congratulations. You made it," James said. *"You will see my image projected on the screen later. I will say hi to you and give you some messages."*

I kept my eyes closed, imagined and waited for this surprise, this *gift*.

Chapter 3

Meng

"Can I have a pen and a piece of paper?" I asked the blue-eyed nurse.

The nurse got a lead pencil and a piece of pink scrap paper on the bedside table. I slowly got up and took them from her and prepared to write. I felt something beneath me was lifting. I thought it was the screen being pulled down from the ceiling. I felt nervous about the sound. It took less than a minute for the nurse to settle me down. I couldn't wait to see James's image arrived on a big white screen in front of my bed.

When I opened my eyes, my husband appeared. He looked at me with a slight smile as if I looked awake in a writing posture. I looked around the ceiling, the curtain divider, the wall.

I was so depressed and disappointed in my husband's presence. I pushed him away and told him to get out of my sight. I was disturbed and irritated by his showing up because he was still a murderer at large. I asked him for my cell phone because I wanted to search for James on the Internet. I tried to know what was going on exactly.

He already had my phone in his hand from the nurse. He turned the power on and gave it to me.

The first thing I did was to Google "James Vidales" and look at all of his images. It took a few seconds before his pictures were spreading out before my eyes. I carefully watched every single related image. He was a productive performance artist developing his career in reality. A picture of him showed him looking like a homeless person, hands crossed, sitting on a chair, wearing a yellow jacket with a brown collar, and surrounding him was a blue cooler, a painting of some sort of pinscher dog, and an oversized red sign that hung on top of his head and read HELP.

He is lonely and helpless, too.

I snapped a shot of the hospital's light green curtain and posted it with the caption on Facebook in a public setting so he would see my message:

> Shake it, tide it, wrap it. It's in the hospital. No kidding. Sneakily got online posting. No kidding. Joke? Break the rule. No one cares about whom.

To let him know that I was in the hospital felt like an accomplishment, like I conquered a mission.

When I finished typing, my husband gave me a delicate eyeglasses case. It was a graceful set of Fendi eyeglasses with crafty floral patterns carved on the arms.

"How do you know my prescription?" I asked.

"I just knew it."

But I'd left the small prescription sheet on the bulletin board after the check-up with my optometrist recently. It was nothing more than that; he was just lucky finding it on the board.

Then he showed me a photo of our daughter on his phone.

"Who is this?" he asked and held it up. "Can you still recognize her?"

I looked at Aisa's chubby cheeks and arms carefully. The way she frowned in the picture looked just like a mini-me.

Is it a mirror?

I was confused about whether it was a mirror or a screen. She looked like the genius inside of me who had died. I pushed away my husband's phone because I was too tired to talk any more.

"Get out of here!" I yelled.

After my husband left, I heard some noises behind the light green curtain. I'd had enough things in disorder.

Who the hell is behind there?

I jumped off the bed and pulled back the curtain.

A girl screamed.

Her appearance terrified me. She looked horrible, with an ugly, pock-marked face. She was pale and sloppy and had a bad smell. I imagined her living here for hundreds of years. Her long black hair was dry and stiff and the same as mine.

What did I create!

I scanned her by walking around her bed—I couldn't believe my eyes. The name on her chart was Meng. Her face resembled a man with a wig. Her eyes were spiritless and squinting. Even with her hunchback, you could still tell that she was tall and robust. She glanced sideways at me while combing her fingers through her hair.

I praised myself: *Very creative! Very creative! She is a grotesque MONSTER!*

I closed the curtain and buried myself in the bedclothes. I felt the world settle around me. The voices of a debate resounded in my ears sonorous and distorted like voices underwater.

"Did she believe that every man would like to have coitus with her?" Death said.

"False," James (God) said. *"She didn't think about every man but me."*

"Did she fail in her attempts to be with you?" said Death.

"………." God pondered.

"She did," said the Death. "She failed to find you by wrongful thoughts. She was thinking about things repeatedly incorrect at every step despite your hints. She thinks to leave her husband and daughter, a pathetic lustful woman undeserving of sympathy." Death grabbed the point and dug in.

"False," said God solemnly. *"Did the fantasy happen? Who stirred her lust? Not her initiative, but the spirits did."*

"What do you mean that the spirits stirred her lust?" Death said.

"By consistently haunting her with voices, by preoccupying her body and will, by stealing her soul and refusing to let her go," God said.

"They all come from her hallucinations, don't they?"

"........." God pondered again—this debate was terminating his job.

I almost cost him his right to be God.

"That is True," said the Death. "Oh James, did you forget who you are? You love her, and so do I. You desired to have her soul, and so do I! But did she manage to DIE? Firstly, she failed her life, and she failed every step that you hinted at—now she is wasting our time. She is a stubborn woman, isn't she?" Death's voice echoed profoundly.

"True," said James after a very long pause. He started to fade and weaken—he was helpless and saddening with sorrow.

Death continued. "Her wrongful thoughts do not qualify her as an angel. I sentenced this woman. Here is where she belongs. The creature that she made will be accompanying her," said Death. "And Gordon is still her husband."

The air fell into silence.

That was not my intention, not my intention! I tried to shake the voices out of my head in my hands.

At night, I felt the lump tingling. It was like a needle stuck in my ass, an unbearable pain if I lay on my back. *I must be in hell now because I don't know how to sleep anymore.* I got off the bed and walked through the darkness of the hall.

A bright room, and through the glass window, was a duty nurse. I sneakily crawled below her line of sight so I could observe what she was. The ground was hard and cold, and that hurt my butt even more, so I went back to the hall to sit on a chair. I heard the nurse sigh and get up, approaching me.

A slim young Asian girl with beautiful talking eyes. She was cute with small prominent cheekbones.

"Hey, are you okay? Do you want some water?" Her was soft and sweet voice.

She gave me a small cup of water, and I complained about my sleeping problem.

"I can't sleep," I said, my tone innocent. "I don't know how to sleep anymore. My constipation is hurting me..."

"Oh dear," she said. "I can give you some pills. Okay?"

A few moments later she handed me two tiny white pills in a paper wrapper.

I lay on the bed after taking the pills. It was a deep sleep, but I was woken by a cry of my nickname from my mom. She sounded like she was underwater, struggling in the dark. I closed my eyes and fell back asleep. I woke up again during the night, this time to the sound of spoken voices. There stood two nurses;

one of them was the chubby robotic nurse. They were discussing something between beds under the dim light.

I'm in the hospital, I thought.

I closed my eyes and felt the root of my tongue rapidly touch the upper jaw, which signalled that someone died somewhere in the world. I have had this kind of reaction so many times that it deprived me of sleep at home, and now it went back again.

The next morning, I woke up with some noises made by my roommate. She banged her hands hard all of a sudden, whispered to herself, and then banged again. It was the banging that woke me. She was not a dummy. I went to check out the window beside her bed and spotted lots of snacks put on her bedside table. Lots of snacks and candies made her mouth look very bad, poorly filled with black gaps and decay:

What kind of alien is this? I was alive as an ordinary person, not knowing how bad a human being could be. I wouldn't be able to endure it if I had this deformity in such a shame of mindless living, and yet she is still surviving.

"Jessie… Jessie… Jessie!" I heard of a woman called my name.

It was the nurse who looked like another senior Angel. I just fell into another deep sleep on a chair in the hall.

"It's time to take your pill." The nurse in her fifties with the long blond hair woke me up and gave me a cup of water and pills that I felt I couldn't take anymore because of the drowsiness.

One evening through my drowsiness, I saw a woman who was drying her long, curly black hair near the nursing station. I wandered the hall and passed by her with a glance, and a flash shone upon her head. I walked around the adjacent rooms, and this woman appeared again.

She is a ghost! I thought.

My brainwaves seemingly connected with the TV sound and heard a lot of intimate chatting just like in the critique class back at graduate school. Jeannie (who was my advisor) and my best friend Chen were talking about James and me. Jeannie always spoke in a firm and calm voice and posed questions with skepticism. Chen would suddenly understand what she said and ask her own questions. They were discussing my situation and commenting on why I had become ill. Why did I crush on James all of a sudden?

Admittedly, I desired a relationship with a kind of communication by just a gaze. The inspiration came from the couple, Dan and Pro. One time, Chen and I went to buy our dinner and saw them eying each other as they sat at the corner in the express Chinese restaurant. After finishing our orders, without hearing any words between them, I saw the tears shed from Pro's beautiful eyes. We passed by the window and saw Dan's eyes socket were red, mouth compressed. I thought they were playing a game, but the reaction was intense and stronger than a kiss, hug, touch, any other body contact but the most direct.

The exercise I did the most in the ward was walking rounds in the hall. After the nursing station, a turn to two shower rooms on the left, the adjacent room was a conference room, then a dead corner to a narrower hallway with many locked rooms on both sides. There were too many cells locked to know what they were used for. The pathway of this labyrinth converged on another hall right behind the nursing room that faced the entrance.

One day, I walked rapidly and scored hundreds of cycles with bare feet: *This body is so sturdy. It can't die, can it?* I could already feel the head was separate from the feet, and they were not mine. The middle-aged nurse with blond hair stopped me.

"I see you have done lots of exercises!" she said. "Sit down and take a rest."

She was the one who woke me up from the chair. She pulled a blood pressure monitor to check me and brought me into a small room to check my weight and height.

Such an outdated and inaccurate way to check the mental state, thought my brain, which was more inclined to trust than my body.

I went back to bed and recognized a familiar person walking towards me.

She is also alive!?

It was my sister Connie, who came to visit me in her eighth month of pregnancy. I went to bed, and my hemorrhoids were killing me when I sat down. Connie brought some food for me.

She didn't say anything but just looked at me with frowning eyes while making a couple of sniffing sounds. She had done this since she was a child. Connie stared at me with a little bit of anger—her poor, mentally disordered younger sister.

"Drink some soup," she said.

I heard a video calling on her phone. It sounded like from another world, somewhere that echoed. Connie started the video call. As soon as my mom saw me in my hospital gown she started sobbing. Our youngest sister was there too, and she cried and grew angry."

"Why did you become like this?"

Wow! They are all still alive!

I pushed away from the phone when I saw myself on the screen and refused to talk. I shook my head to Connie, so she ended the call without any further communication. Connie left me with the soup.

When she left, I walked over to Meng who was in my next bed.

"Can I have some?" I pointed a bunch of snacks on her table. Meng nodded and put the bites on her bed. I picked the seaweed pack and went out to the hall.

That was a sunny afternoon with the sound of the TV. I enjoyed eating the seaweed and held the last piece against the sun. It looked like a beautiful shiny green agate that was stunning with the hollows in it. I thought of a boy I met when I was still a youth, and I still remember his name—Wei Yi Wang.

I knew him from the art studio. He had tried to talk to me:

"It seems like it would kill you to open your mouth to talk," he said and watched me sketching his still life.

I didn't reply. He always wore a cobalt blue top and sometimes would play a blue electronic guitar. He had a kind of distinctive odour that would remain after he left. A scent I wouldn't fail to catch if I smelled it. I was curious about its source. Once his image appeared as Death and claimed my life, too.

Could he also be in this place?

The world would be flipping over once I put this last slice of seaweed through the sun. I tilted it and looked at the hollows changing with the sunlight as looking through a kaleidoscope.

Chapter 4

Zen

The next morning, when I entered the narrow hallway, there was a room that made a quivering sound. I twisted my ears to listen, and a roaring sound occurred behind the door.

James had an affinity with a nurse inside. He gazed at me with a triumphant smile.

There were days when I walked passing by that room that I thought it might be a wormhole that could dispatch me to another world. I decided to open the door, but it was locked. The vibration didn't stop.

I was excited about what I discovered.

"It's a wormhole! A wormhole exists inside," I whispered to myself.

Passing by the balcony, I saw the curly black-haired woman was rambling about in her gown. I went out there and wondered about her. I noticed her tanned skin, thin but fit. I felt solid after I saw her bare feet, not a spirit after all. I overheard the birds chirping while walking with her in a circuit. The outside was much more withdrawn.

"Can I speak to you?" I asked and noticed her peacefully crossed her hands at the front of her chest.

"Yeah, sure!" she said with a friendly voice.

"What brought you here?" I said.

"Something fell to me," she said.

I realized her quick walking pace made me the illusion.

After a silence I pressed on. "Do you work?" I decided to change the topic because of the reserve.

"Yes. I offered lectures at the university," she replied.

"What was the subject?"

"It's continuing education of biology," she replied.

"You must be very knowledgeable," I responded.

"So here I am," she stated.

I laughed at her answer. "So your students take the class at night?" I asked.

"That's right."

"Who were the students?" I asked.

"Coming from everywhere, businessmen, doctors, teachers…"

She then lectured about her research on the relationship of molecule and biology for a while. I was perplexed by her subject a little bit.

"What brought you here?" She asked.

"Because of a man," I said. "I fell in love with him, but I'm married."

"Who is he?" she said.

"He was my classmate from a long time ago," I replied.

"You can let him know that you miss him. You want to keep in touch with him, you know." She picked up the dark blue towel from the brick ground. "Let's go inside to talk."

We kept on roaming, yet within my circuit this time. I saw her towel draped on the shoulder. She had a unique temperament that soothed people. I couldn't imagine any aberration in her, and I knew that she wouldn't tell me.

"What's your name?" I asked.

"Zen," she replied.

"Are you married?"

"No," she said. "I have only a boyfriend."

"How is he?"

"He is charming. I love him. It's been five years with him, and we are still getting along well." Zen grinned as though her boyfriend were walking right beside her.

"Where is he from?"

"He was a Mestizo," said Zen. "Some of his ancestors were European."

When we crossed near the room that made the mysterious noises, the door was still rocking. The coitus was still going on. I felt embarrassed for them—the racing thoughts of paranoid romantic episode made sense to me at that moment.

"How about your husband?" asked Zen. "How is your relationship with him?"

"We are okay." I was quiet for a moment. "I'm thinking about a split."

I felt inspired by what I said because I hadn't thought about divorce. "I mean, just thinking. We have a daughter,"

"Doing what you feel happy about is the most important thing in life, isn't it?" said Zen.

A Caucasian doctor with a blue and white checked shirt walked by. He didn't wear any uniform, but people could still immediately tell he was a doctor by his temperament. He was a blue-eyed sir with a friendly smile. I saw him walk into a room at the back of the hall. The other day when I went to see the black nameplate on the door, the golden convex fonts engraved on the door read: DR. JAMES HUFFMAN.

"What big deal about sex in a relationship?" I continued to say.

"It's one of the most crucial things in a relationship," she said. "To me anyway it is the most important thing in life."

I drew courage from what she had said.

"Can you believe I had only sex with my husband once since we were married and got pregnant?"

"Wow! I can't believe it! I can't imagine! No wonder you want a split!" She seemed shocked, but I liked her reaction.

In truth it was not *only* one time, but we soon took up birth control. We made love a couple of times in successive nights—one unpleasant experience spread over a few nights.

But was a split the only answer to this difficulty?

My husband came to visit me again.

This time, I asked to use his cell phone because mine was dead in the nurse's storage box. James must have seen the message I posted on Facebook by then. I searched his name via Google images and scrolled over the pictures of his artworks:

He wore the cowboy boots covered with knives; he hugged and danced with a girl with long, straight black hair like me under the dim light; he was cocooned in a coonskin cap, smirking; he shaved his moustache with a bowie knife and gazed at me.

The messages had scattered to the world that he loved me and was struggling for me through the appearance on the Internet. He posed against a wall with red human-shaped target dots, naked, with arms opened with the legend below the picture:

"The Great God Pan Is Dead."

I was astounded by this image because it solidly proved that his voices, the Angel—the circumstances that happened—were present. Could this connection be a coincidental match? I never sought his artwork until now except for the serape.

My brain spontaneously generated a story that he fell in the old timer's era. He sacrificed himself as a God for me in his past life.

I then searched his Facebook and messaged:

Hi, how are you?

Getting in touch with an old classmate, what's the big deal? I gave the phone back to my husband. It is going to be another seductive game—I closed my eyes and knew that the myth hadn't ended.

In the bathroom, I rinsed my mouth, and a deep sound like a wolf's cry came up from my throat. The sink echoed. My body shivered after the unexpected roar. The image of Gucci bolting with the black spirits appeared. There was a wolf inside of my body hunting for the soul of Gucci, my husband's beloved dog. He didn't want to leave my body because he was not tamed yet. I closed my perceptions when I sat on the potty. James held an antler cane, wore a coonskin huntsman hat with abundant furs and stared at the creatures in my body. By the time James's huntsman image appeared, the spirits that cluttered in my body were in fear and trembled. James symbolized an agreement among all of us and declared:

"WE are asking the spirits residing in Jessie's body to go away—SHE is this body's dominator. Either agree with her beliefs, root and deed, or begone."

I am begging you to leave, (Jessie) thought.

"Jessie…" said the she-wolf who remained in her body despite the warning; her intentions were marked, her spirit more intense, her brain resolute that all of these stories should be written down one day.

Part Two

Chapter 5

Weiwei

When she woke up the morning, sun shone through the windows, and Jessie heard Meng's snoring. She got up and explored the ward. Passing by a well-lit room, she saw a chubby Asian girl, Weiwei, who seemed to be packing her belongings on the bed. It was a single room that Jessie wanted, so she asked her if she could move in. Weiwei kindly said yes and that she would ask the nurse if the room was available. Jessie sat down and felt the bed was more comfortable than hers. It made her think of coming back to school days.

The next morning while Jessie was strolling around, she bumped into Weiwei. When Jessie approached her with yesterday's question, Weiwei seemed shocked and nervously walked into the room, then she rushed, running out to the end of the hallway where the entrance was. She bent down and rapidly drew a line across floor between Jessie and herself. She looked like she was plotting something or drawing a clear boundary.

She must be offended by yesterday's question, Jessie thought and felt laughable about Weiwei and herself.

Connie came to visit her with her husband, Peter, and their daughter, Daisy. Peter looked at her on the bed empathetically and told her to recover very soon. Her five-year-old niece, Daisy, jumped up on her bed and accidentally touched the buttons on the side. Daisy stopped at once, afraid that she'd made a big mistake.

"Look! If you press this button, the bed will be lifted up!" Jessie said as the bed hoisted her up little by little.

It was the sound that she thought was the screen being pulled down from the ceiling. Daisy was so happy about permission (and the fun discovery) that she jumped onto the bed to play with Jessie.

"You got to go travel somewhere with Gordon," said Peter, "so that you don't feel so depressed! You know?"

"Do you know where San Diego is?" said Jessie.

"Sure," he said. "Take some time with Gordon, just you and him alone for fun! You became sick because you have nothing to do at home."

"Yeah! I will book the plane ticket to San Diego," she said.

Connie didn't say a word but looked worried and annoyed with her big belly. Her due date was one month away in June.

Soon it was six o'clock and dinnertime. Jessie looked at her reflection in the window glass. A whispering appeared at the door:

"Look! Who is there?"

It was her mother-in-law holding her daughter, Aisa. They'd gotten permission from the hospital, so mother and daughter could see each other. Carefully walking towards Jessie, her mother-in-law smiled, Jessie and Aisa hadn't seen each other for almost a month.

"It's Mommy!" Grandma said excitedly. "Call your mom!"

Aisa stared at Jessie confusedly. It reminded Jessie of when she had first cut her hair short, and Aisa had curiously stared at her like she was a stranger. She started to cry and touched the tears on her cheeks with small chubby fingers. The same pair of eyes, but with fear and sadness.

"Baby..." Jessie called her daughter with her hands opened.

Aisa swiftly turned away but later put her forehead on her grandma's neck, tilted to peek at Jessie. She was unsure of this woman who felt so familiar and yet so strange and was called Mom. She was almost one and a half years old but had become so mature—her hair longer, which made her look more sophisticated.

Jessie thought Grandma would be such an excellent caregiver for Aisa that she was not even needed. The idea of separation came to her mind again.

"Okay," said Grandma. "We've got to go. It's dinner time! Mommy needs to eat now!"

Jessie watched them leave.

While eating the dinner, she looked around all in-patients with the same gown and saw a young bearded Middle Eastern man looking at her. The meal was beef with brown sauce. She usually didn't like cooked beef, but it tasted just right, tender and mild with the sauce.

The first male in-patient she talked about was Dawson. He was a fiftyish Caucasian with silver hair and red cheeks; he had big blue eyes and a loud voice. He was asking the nurse for his sleeping pills. He looked spiritual and smart when he talked. Jessie was watching TV in the corner that day. Dawson came and adjusted the TV stand to be closer to him and sat down with her.

"Do you mind if I change it?" he said with his hand about to touch the buttons on the TV.

Jessie shook her head and embraced her knees which shifted her weight a bit; her bottom still ached. The channels stopped at on sports. Dawson touched his nose with his hand and made sniffing noises quite often and his legs muscle, fingers, arms, and shoulders, everywhere would twitch periodically.

"Are you okay?" she said.

"Oh! I'm fine," he said with a series of anxiety-provoking twitches.

After some minutes of silence, she turned to him.

"You know, my bottom hurts! There was a lump on my anus. It just doesn't go away."

He looked down at her. "Do you want me to push it in for you?" he asked and held up two fingers.

She slowly shook her head. Meanwhile, a young Asian man in a light-yellow gown came in. He was pale and had bloodshot eyes and longish hair and looked like he'd just woken up. He aggressively pushed the TV stand against the wall. Jessie moved her spot to the side.

"Don't change it," Dawson said, his voice loud and assertive. "Leave it on."

The young man with a pair of bloodshot and weary eyes lunged in between them. Jessie got up right away and left. Two other in-patients came in: the chubby Asian girl, talking with a tall, lean, tanned Asian boy. He saw Jessie. His eyes were strangely unfocussed and looked weird, like you wouldn't know who he spoke to.

Perhaps he was the God in blind.

The chubby Asian girl stepped forward.

"The two of you can be good friends," she said.

Jessie didn't say anything and simply walked away. Eileen, the occupational therapist, was the one who wrote on the board outside of the nursing station letting people know the time and number of people who could go to the garden outside for a walk. She had seen a group of in-patients come back before. Jessie went up and asked her if she could also go. Eileen smiled at her.

"Jessie, I don't have you on the list yet. I will check another day."

The next morning Jessie went to the balcony to find Zen, but she was not there. Jessie tried to open the door to access the balcony a couple of times, but it didn't work. The door seemed locked. She sat down on a chair by the exit door and looked at the table soccer in the hall. She closed her eyes and heard a loud voice—the Middle Eastern young man opened the door.

Is he God? Jessie wondered and got up to look for Zen.

While she was walking around the hall, passing by the wards, she peeked in at the ward that Zen had come out of the other day. But the room was empty. After a couple of circuits, she saw the Asian man with uncanny eyes sitting on a chair in the hall. She went to sit with him. He held a black cassette player and listened with black earbuds.

Which century does he live in?

She took a close look at his eyes.

"Are you blind?" she asked.

The young man looked at her with unfocused eyes and quickly shook his head. Jessie waved her hands in front of his eyes.

"Can you see for real?"

The young man nodded. He had angular cheeks and stump moustache on his upper lip and chin.

"Can I listen, too?" Jessie said.

The young man gave her one earbud. She heard a male singer singing an old Cantonese song. Once she would have turned off this type of music, but she didn't that day. The young man suddenly snatched a kiss on her cheek. She was surprised and gave him back the earbud. She could still feel his wet quivering lips on her cheek. She got up and walked away.

The next day, Jessie saw the young man who kissed her dressed in casual clothes and listening to his cassette in the TV hall. She sat down, and he offered her one earbud again. But Jessie shook her head. Later she saw him carrying luggage in the hall. The nurse had a conversation with an older man who was picking him up. It was his father. That was the last time she saw him.

The chubby Asian girl was also gone.

When Gordon visited, she asked for his cell phone. She was sitting on the bed and couldn't wait to check if her message to James had got a reply. When she opened Messenger, she saw her message was still there—the word *Seen* displayed beneath her message with a timestamp. She typed another message and sent:

I love you when I am sitting down.

She was hopeful that James would respond after this message because he had seen the last text, and that was something, wasn't it? At least he knew it even without replying. She turned off the phone and gave it back to Gordon. He gave her a pair of thick plastic-framed spectacles that she asked him to get from her drawer. She wore them and left the Fendi spectacles on the table.

After Gordon left, she brought a white towel with her to the balcony and found the door was easy to push open. Spreading the towel on the hot brick ground and lying on top, she closed her eyes, feeling the wind on her face, blowing gently, the sun filtering continuously through the gap between the leaves, scattered over a ground shade, sunshine, ants, lingering on the ground. The beeping sound from the pedestrian light down at the street persistently repeatedly calling:

ti-so... ti-so... ti-so... ti-so...

It lasted around a minute and merged with the sound of a couple of seagulls screaming. It was a sunny sky with clouds moving slowly. It was an uneventful afternoon but served as one of the best days in Jessie's life.

Chapter 6

Ikhlas

From the doctor's medical report:

> *With this treatment of antipsychotic medication, risperidone, starting from a very low dose of 0.5 mg, the patient responded slowly first, and later the dosage was increased further up to 5 mg a day. This relatively heavy dose of antipsychotics for a relatively small oriental woman finally kicked in with substantial improvement level. She became social in the ward, attended different activities, became more talkative, expressive with emotions and was able to make sense. The delusions and hallucinations, ideas of references gradually shrunk and then disappeared...*

"Jessie! You have been outside too long! Come on in!"

Woken by a nurse's shout at the door, she picked up her towel and went inside. A few patients were sitting in the hall, eating. She saw one meal tray left on the cart covered with the foil. The in-patients here looked normal and healthy, none of them looked like prisoners nor patients who seemed ill. Jessie felt that she lived her life together with a group of people who were occupied mindfully. They were chilled, chaste, concentrated psychics. The young Middle Eastern man was Ikhlas, and he passed by her and walked to the balcony.

There was an old man, and an old woman resting on the chairs when she sat down in the hall. They were sitting in the distance, but you could still tell they had a connection. The old man held his hands resting atop his cane and looked at Jessie. The image of this couple sitting together as a large gilt-framed mirror that depicted something.

Are they Gordon and me after sixty years? she thought.

There was a man with spectacles—tall and with robust embonpoint—talking to himself lingeringly walking behind the couple. He snapped his fingers and came to sit down beside Jessie, whispering plausibly to himself. He wore a carefully trimmed black moustache, and it made him kind of like James, a chubby version.

"Do you have a girlfriend?" asked Jessie.

He looked at her over his thick shoulder. "I have a fiancée."

"Where is she?" she said.

"She is in Europe, travelling," he said. "We are going to get married next month."

"Nice," said Jessie. "Why doesn't she come to see you?"

"I don't know. She disappeared before I was sent here," said the man and got up.

She sought a friend who could talk to her as Zen had. It seemed like not many in-patients lived in the unit after Zen left. That day, she saw an old woman with spectacles come out from a room bright with big windows. She had a tanned complexion, a round head and nose, and pronounced cheekbones. Jessie approached her.

"Can I talk to you?"

"Yes," said the woman.

The woman's name was Olena, and in the afternoon, walking a little while in the hall with the lights off, Jessie broke the silence between them.

"Why are you here?" she asked.

"I was abandoned by my husband," said the woman.

"How did that happen?" said Jessie.

"He hated me. He hit me and ran away, so my brother and sister put me here."

The old woman looked like an innocent lamb, and Jessie felt pity for her. Their conservation was lagging as sorely as their walking feet.

"Why are you here?" asked the old woman.

"I would divorce from my husband," said Jessie.

"Why?"

"I am not happy with him."

Jessie felt what she said was somehow untenable compared to what the woman told about her life situation.

"Where are you from?" asked Jessie.

"I am from the Philippines," said the old woman and checked the time on her golden watch. "I need to go to take my medicine."

The watch made Jessie feel nostalgic. She once gave her mother a similar watch that had made her mother happy. Jessie went into the ward with her. There were two beds, but Imelda was the only one who lived here. Jessie squatted against the wall and waited for her. It took a few minutes, and they went back to walk again.

"I like your hand," said Jessie.

The old woman held up her hand and laughed.

"Your hand looks just like my mom's. Do you mind if I hold your hand?" said Jessie.

"I don't mind," she said.

They held hand together and walked in the hall a little while.

There was a surprise visitor who came to see her that day—her father-in-law. She gave him a big hug as he opened his arms already when he saw her in the hall.

"How are you? Do you feel better?" he said.

Jessie nodded and felt kind of embarrassed by her morbidity. Her father-in-law was followed by her mother-in-law. They went to the balcony to talk.

"I am going to call your mom to discuss your situation," said her father-in-law as he sat on the bench.

Through speakerphone the conversation sounded like nothing to do with her. She squatted on the ground to see the ants crawling. Later, her father-in-law gave her the phone to talk with her mom privately.

"We are booking the plane ticket to see you, okay? Be well. I know you are not sick. You just have been overthinking, alright? Be good. You will get better soon. Daddy also believes that you are not ill. I went to ask the fortune teller about your thing, and he said you have had a bizarre life—the man who you should meet didn't appear, but you met a businessman. The man who did not show might be a politician, a very stubborn and strong-willed man... I told them that you are just too romantic, having all those ridiculous thoughts..."

After she finished her speech, she said goodbye to Jessie, and they hung up.

It was a piece of exciting news, Jessie thought. *James might be the man.*

The next day, Jessie saw Dawson playing poker alone at the table in the hall. She was attracted by the cards and sat down.

"I saw you went out yesterday," said Jessie.

He'd worn a blue and white checked shirt and had looked refreshed coming back from outside. Apparently, he didn't sleep in the ward at night. He must have the privilege offered by the hospital to do so. Big two—a popular Chinese card game—wasn't much fun playing with only two players, so Jessie asked the Filipino woman to sit down and play with them.

"I went to visit friends," he said.

Jessie won a couple of rounds with luck.

"I am going to win this time!" Dawson said and looked at Jessie carefully trying to guess her cards by the look on her face.

After the dinner, Dawson asked her if she'd like to watch a movie. He pushed the chunky TV stand to the hall. By the time she came out of the ward, the lights were all turned off. She sat down with Dawson for a little while, but the soundtrack of the movie—*Signs* with Mel Gibson—panicked her. The mysterious atmosphere and long periods of silence, suddenly interrupted by a flash of noise, brought her fear back. She went behind the TV to see if there was anything hidden there. She saw three people were sitting side by side in the dark together without talking. Ikhlas sat between a man and a grey turbaned woman. They looked like his parents.

She was scared of looking at the wall in front of her bed under the dim yellow light.

The next day when they played poker, they had a more extended conversation and spoke of insignificant things in their lives that both of them would likely forget.

"My girlfriend is Asian, too," said Dawson. "She is very clever."

Dawson told the nurse who just passed by him not to forget to give him sleeping pills.

"Do you need sleeping pills to sleep every day?" asked Jessie.

"Oh yeah, of course," said Dawson. "Every day!"

"Can I come to your place to play cards after I'm discharged?" asked Jessie.

"Yeah. I live with my girlfriend in the condo on No. 3 Road in Richmond."

The next day Jessie intentionally checked Dawson's ward, the single room that he had with his own desk and chair. In there she had seen him playing the cribbage alone, and that had made her feel like he was controlling electric power somewhere in the world by that little device that she never saw. But Jessie hasn't seen him for a while, and all of his stuff for killing time—the crossword page on the newspaper, cribbage board, pen and book—were still left on the table. She was bored and sat on the chair. Ikhlas came to sit down with her.

She was happy to see him because she felt he looked like another version of James with bushy sideburns and a moustache even though he was way younger. They stared at each other first, but she was so timid that she dropped her whole body from the chair and looked at him upside down. She would like to know if he would change to another look if she saw him at this angle. Her hands crossed over her chest, and her long hair fell off the chair that touched the floor.

"Jessie…" said Ikhlas with a helpless tone of voice.

How did he know my name? This question aroused her interest in him.

"Jessie, your husband!" said the nurse.

Jessie jumped up from the chair. Gordon came to visit her and brought her something to eat. Asking for his phone, Jessie checked if her message had been replied by James. He had, however, seen it but without any reply. The word *seen* already meant a lot for her, so she sent a picture of her daughter wearing a fake moustache and glasses with the text:

She looked just like you.

…and returned the phone to Gordon.

That was six o'clock dinner. After Gordon left, she strolled around the wards with her tummy full of food that Gordon brought to her.

The next sunny morning, as she lay on the towel on the balcony, Ikhlas came. She kept her eyes closed and didn't say anything. He sat down on the bench next to her.

"Do you like here, too?" asked Jessie with eyes closed.

The beeping sound from the pedestrian's traffic light loudly emerged.

"Yep," said Ikhlas.

"Me, too," said Jessie. A few seagulls screamed nearby.

"Can we go inside to talk?" he asked.

It sounded like an order, but she got up to follow him. When they walked around the hall, she found the room with the shaky door and now realized that it was a heater inside that made a series of rumbling noises.

"I am married," said Jessie, with hands crossed while walking.

"I know," he said.

"Do you believe in God?" said Jessie.

"I testify there is no God other than God," said Ikhlas.

"Do you have a girlfriend?" she said.

"I have many friends who are girls," he said.

"That means you have a good relationship with girls," said Jessie who sounded, just then, like a mom or a teacher.

"I also like to play computer games with boys if you are talking about the relationship," he said.

"What kind of game do you play with boys?" she said.

"I would play any as long as my boy friends like," he said.

"You are a kind man," she said and felt a chill crawling throughout her body as their walking pace quickened.

"Don't you feel cold?" she said and draped the towel that she just brought over his shoulders.

She found his body was also shivering a bit. That made her feel she was more powerful than him, although she misunderstood him—he was psionic when he pushed out the locked door of the balcony. She grabbed a towel from the rack and gave it to him.

"Can we slow down?" she said.

After they passed by the nursing station, the hall to the middle of the hallway, he turned to her.

"Can I hug you?"

Jessie stopped and nodded. She watched his chest as they embraced, her face and breast pressed into him. He smelled like a stuffy wool ball.

The hug lasted ten seconds. It was a firm and assertive touch that they could leave apart forever.

"Feel better?" she said.

"Yep," he said. "Can I have your phone number so we can keep in touch after we leave here?"

"Yes, let me get a pen and paper from my room."

Jessie walked to her ward with Ikhlas following behind. Jessie waved him in.

"I am sorry, but I am not allowed to enter another patient's room," he said and stood still at the door.

Jessie smiled and wrote down her phone number and gave it to him.

Soon after, Jessie saw her mother-in-law's head appear at the window of the entrance door. In the hallway to the entrance, Jessie squatted down, waiting until the nurse buzzed the bell to let the door open.

Aisa saw Jessie squatted there waiting with opened arms and ran to her.

"Mommy!"

Jessie held her up tightly. They spent a little while in the hall; last time she'd brought Aisa to play in the balcony for a while, but the nurse warned her mother-in-law that Jessie was not allowed to stay alone with Aisa yet. When Jessie played the piano, she heard Aisa call her mother-in-law *Mom* many times. Her mother-in-low corrected her every time.

"Mom is there!" she would say. "Look! That's Mom playing the piano."

Jessie stopped playing, closed the lid and turned back to hug Aisa.

I have to leave here. I am losing her, thought Jessie.

It was a very sunshiny noon. She just finished her lunch but didn't see Ikhlas. She went into his ward and found him sleeping. Jessie approached him to see if he was just closing his eyes meditatively. It was a sound, deep sleep, and his face looked so peaceful. That was the last time she saw Ikhlas.

Chapter 7

Brian

"Do you want some?" said Brian, the young Asian man with the light-yellow gown.

Once he'd merely offered her a cookie when they sat together watching TV, but not today. Jessie had rejected him by shaking her head to the cookie he put at the front of her face, but Brian forcefully rammed it into her firm closed lips. Without saying any words, the weatherman in a dark blue suit on TV soaked wet by the tears that hovering in her eyes. With some cookie crumbs, the searing pain on her lips lasted for a while. She wished Dawson could be there.

She wandered around in the hallway and saw Brian's mom buzz the doorbell outside. A quiet Asian woman who often visited the hospital slowly came inside.

"Why are you coming again?" said Brian, putting his legs on the table. "I hate you! Get out of here! I don't know you!"

He walked away and roared in the hallway. His mom still remained quiet and sat in the hall. A nurse went to talk with Brian.

There was a new female inmate. Olena was Ukrainian with short curly reddish hair. Jessie saw her strolling around the hall and leaned towards her.

"Oh my God, you are so beautiful," Olena said, "like an angel!"

Olena got along well with Brian right away. Both of them had the same craziness and similar characteristics: rebellion, irritable, and aggressive. She interrupted Jessie's drawing activity and called her to go with her. Three of them walked behind the nursing station. On the way entering the narrow hallway, Olena pointed to the far end.

"There is a camera there. Come." She brought Brian and Jessie to the dead corner where Ikhlas hugged Jessie. "Here has no camera. You can kiss, smoke, and do whatever you want, you know?"

She left them after this conversation.

Jessie continued to stroll with Brian.

"How are you doing?" he asked in Mandarin.

"I'm okay," said Jessie.

"We can be good friends," he said.

"Do you remember last time you forced me to eat your cookie," said Jessie.

"Oh yeah! I'm so sorry," he said. "So sorry about that."

After a short silence, Jessie went back to her drawing, but she got called by the therapist Eileen for a session of a group meeting. The first meeting she went to was about healthy food. Eileen wanted the patients to give her the names of some food considered healthy.

After writing "apple" with a blue marker on the whiteboard, she turned around.

"What else do you think is healthy for your body?" she said with pursed lips.

She had a full head of short wavy, glistening white hair, and crossed her hands on her chubby body and lay back in the chair like she was the boss.

Emerging on-and-off sudden loud drilling noises from the next room.

"How about you lose some weight first and then talk about it?" said James.

Jessie burst into laughs at the randomness of the comment! She couldn't believe what she had just heard and couldn't stopping giggle her head off at the table. An Asian girl, Karen, who sat in front of her, began to laugh when she saw Jessie laugh. That brought Jessie back to her school days. Eileen seemed very used to the madness and still talked very vigorously—her bloody red pearl earrings swaying while two girls restrained their laughs at the front seats.

"Make love with me." The rumbled drilling sound brought out James again. *"I want to fuck you!"*

She was afraid that Karen would hear his voice because the sounds were getting louder.

Stop, James! Her grins fading gradually and helplessly shook her head.

The other meeting Jessie went to involved a bracelet-making activity. Eileen taught them how to use a stick to make the narrowed newspaper strips into small rolls. The colours and textures of beads she chose from the box were golden, metal, and wooden, which created an original style of combination with the black and white newspaper curl-up beads.

"Look at Jessie's bracelet! She is a very artsy person," Eileen said to the other occupational therapist, Susan.

Since Eileen's compliments, Jessie worked on a mandala every day. She was the only one who would draw in the hall. Most of them stayed in their wards and slept for the whole day. Olena called her to chat with her sometimes. She told Jessie a lot of stories about herself and how nice her husband treated her and her daughter. Jessie was a patient listener. Olena looked at her and said:

"Your hair is so beautiful! I wish I had hair like yours."

Jessie thought that perhaps it wasn't her appearance but her normality (compared to the other patients) that made Olena keep praising and admiring her. That was one of the reasons Jessie couldn't reject this rambunctious woman—because he saw something inside of Jessie.

In the afternoon, Brian put his legs against the wall and talked on the phone at the booth with the newspaper spread on his lap. Sometimes he browsed an article in the paper after a phone call. He looked like he was searching for a job. This was a telephone provided for the patients—the only way to connect with the outside world. Today, Jessie was drawing a mandala while waiting to use the phone.

Jessie noticed Brian was harassing people. He'd murmur on the phone then hang up angrily. He conceived of himself as a hero and planned out something to save the world. To get his scheme done required a lot of text marked up in the newspaper—these were clues—especially the politically related news. Jessie understood. The plots in his brain must have their own logic that no one could dismantle. She saw him finally finish up his phone calls and become engrossed again in his research on the table with a pen again.

"You know, our phone is bugged," he said with a whisper to Jessie.

Jessie nodded.

"I am still piecing the clues together," he said, "but I already phoned the secretary of the Russian president."

Jessie laughed out loud.

"Brian, let's go for your CT scan," said a male nurse pushing a wheelchair. He was the one who looked like Jack Nicholson and did Jessie's CT scan as well. Jessie was more awoken by seeing him now.

"To check if there's a cat in my brain?" said Brian with a tease. He turned to Jessie as he stood up. "What I just said is for real!" he muttered.

"Brian!" the nurse said, hurrying him up.

"Putin loved me," said Jessie as if it were a secret code.

Brian grinned loudly on the way out.

Jessie kind of liked him now. She felt he had a good sense of humour in his own "fabricated" world—just like her—a boy version of herself, both of them had the similarity of nerve, lively imagination, cold on the outside but passionate inside. He was definitely more offensive but wild. Threatening but hilarious. It required a new way to apprehend him.

He was one of the most regular people that Jessie talked to. He also loved to hear information about Jessie's daughter.

"She must be as cute as you," he would say.

The colours that Jessie used on her geometrical mandalas were getting more complex, and the colours were vivid as violet and would pop to people's eyes. There was an old Chinese woman who she once saw sitting with the other man in the hall; she came to talk to her.

"Little girl, you have been here for too long," she said in Mandarin.

Jessie gave her a smile.

"Don't be here for any longer. Here for you is a waste!" She looked at Jessie's drawing.

"Why are you here then?" said Jessie.

"Because I couldn't help suspecting that my husband had another woman!"

Jessie saw her nose had started bleeding. That made her look poorly and near death. Her intuition was right—the man who sat two seats apart from her the other day was her husband.

Jessie went to the telephone booth and called Gordon.

"How are you doing?" she said.

"Pretty good," he said.

"What is baby doing?"

"She is fine, playing with Grandma."

"I want to leave here now," she said.

"Are you finally having enough of all that?" he laughed.

"Can you check my bank account," she asked, "and tell me the balance?"

"Your salary was deposited every month," he said.

She paused for a moment.

"Can I tell you something?" she said. "I want a divorce."

There was a brief pause on the line.

"Okay," he said.

Jessie felt a little bit unreal about his calm tone.

"I will move out first," she said.

"The doctor said you won't be able to recover," he said.

"That's okay," she said. "I can live by myself."

"My mom also said that you should have your own room," said Gordon. "Don't worry about living expenses or rental. I will pay for it if you really want to move out."

Jessie couldn't argue anymore. They always thought ahead of her, and everything was arranged positively. Splitting might be still the best option for them for now. They both hung up the phone. It didn't sound like a joke. Last time, after her father-in-law's visit, Gordon has a short talk with her in the balcony:

"I wish I could be you," he'd said.

"Why?"

"Spending time completely with yourself, isolated from the world, isn't it nice?"

"Do you think I am successful?" she'd asked.

"You are. You are always more successful than me," he'd said, and Jessie just took his words as encouragement for a fast recovery from her illness.

Ever since then, Jessie would call Gordon more often but mainly about Aisa.

Her wardmate was changed to another Asian girl. The last time she saw the candy girl before she moved out was in the hall. She'd had the earphones on her head. This new Asian girl was pale and plump with big eyes like a famous Chinese actress. She was very quiet and didn't even respond to her parents.

They came to stay with her until very late in the first couple of nights. Under the dim light, her father prayed for her until midnight. The dim light made Jessie think of when she was a child, for there was a room as shadowy as this in her grandfather's house.

At midnight, after her grandfather used the toilet, he came to check Connie and Jessie sleeping in the next room. Young Jessie was awakened by the noise. Lying back to the mosquito net in the summertime, she felt him open the net, and his fingers were touching her short pants and panties. Time seemed to freeze at the moment, the uncomfortable touching paralyzed Jessie. Her grandfather didn't go any further.

One time, when Jessie was a teenager, she was taking a shower at home and sensed something over head—a kneeling black figure disappeared like a flash when she put her head up to see the window over the top of the bathroom. She heard her mom, who was also taking a shower upstairs, shout to her dad to get something for her. There seemed a bolt of lightning hit her brain. It was her father peeking in at her in the shower.

Now, in her ward, Jessie did not take any peace or comfort from the prayers of her wardmate's father—and the pale-yellow wall became a hidden hole after he turned off the light.

The next day when she came from outside to use the washroom, she heard this girl talking to the nurse about constipation. There was a foul, putrid stench inside when she wanted to use the toilet. She saw some charcoal black feces stuck in the water. The same smell if you hadn't pooped for too long.

She heard this girl was severely bullied in the school.

One day, Jessie linked her new roommate's arm and walked to Brian. He was watching TV.

"Let's go make friends with him," said Jessie.

The girl stopped when they were about to approach him.

"Don't be shy!" said Jessie.

Jessie felt that she could help someone out before she left here, but the girl was too shy to talk with Jessie as well. But the next morning, Jessie saw her and Brian sitting together in the balcony in the distance. They looked just like Ikhlas and her. Jessie looked out the window and smiled.

Jessie had several meetings with the doctor who wrote her diagnosis. He asked her several questions regarding her hallucinations:

"Have you heard of any strange voice or seen strange things recently?" he asked.

"No."

"Have you had any thoughts about harming yourself or other people?" he asked.

"No."

"Did you take the medication punctually?" he asked.

"Yes," said Jessie. "When can I leave the hospital?"

"Very soon," said the doctor giving her a smile. "You are doing well."

> **The patient did well on short passes, and later long passes were offered to her. Her husband was interviewed at different times. Day passes were all accompanied by the husband. The husband informed us that his mother came to help with the daughter. The patient did well in her relationship with her daughter on the passes. The daughter was quite excited to see the mother. Ministry of Family and Social Services were informed and updated about the patient's improvement. Case references arranged. Home-based**

treatment attended and discussion around the patient's safety, the patient's daughter's safety, and the rest of the family's safety were explored and discussed in detail. It became apparent that the patient has improved significantly, does not have any delusions and hallucinations, has no homicidal or suicidal thoughts and plans, and has enough insight about the nature of her disorder and the importance of the medication. Both the patient and husband agreed that the patient sees home-based treatment after discharged and later to follow with the Richmond Mental Health team, the caseworker, the psychiatrist, and also see the family physician if he needed to or use the Emergency of the hospital in case, she experiences any crisis. The importance of safety was extensively emphasized. The patient's husband felt very solid about the patient's discharge. After the extensive multidisciplinary meeting with the patient, husband, home-based treatment, the social worker.

Chapter 8

The Transient Coma

Jessie was finally discharged by the hospital. Did she miss walking around the hospital, watching the mother duck (Eileen) lead the ducklings (the in-patients) down to the moat? No. And she wouldn't miss being called "idiot" by a man who passed by her.

The first thing she did on the way home was to turn on her phone and check Messenger. But when she opened their conversation window, there was an error, and she couldn't find his profile anymore.

The first night at home, Jessie lay on the bed with Aisa; she lifted up her shirt, and Aisa naturally approached her breast to suck. She had not breastfed her since the hospitalization. She felt something slowly came out inside of her nipple and heard Aisa's suckling sounds. While she'd been hospitalized, Gordon had moved to his mom's house. It was another unfamiliar bed for Jessie, so she had a hard time falling asleep again. The sleeping pills didn't work at all. She needed to go back to see the psychiatrist twice a week, and the social worker would come to visit her every weekend. She was still thinking about divorce from Gordon.

"Where are the papers I need to sign?" asked Jessie.

"Do you really mean it, though?" said Gordon disappointedly.

There was an unread text message from an unknown number from days ago.

> Do you want to come out? I am at Starbucks downstairs in the hospital.

It was Ikhlas. She messaged him back.

> Let me ask my husband.

Gordon was cooking in the kitchen. She asked him if she could go out with a wardmate who was waiting (even though that message was already days ago). Gordon didn't want her to go. Ikhlas never replied.

In the morning, Aisa went to find Jessie in the room. She just came back with Gordon and Grandma. Gordon saw Jessie slackly lying on the bed, so he jumped on her, violently took off her pants and underwear.

"All you need is a fuck!"

He forcedly put his cock in her pussy, and Jessie screamed.

"Stop!"

She heard Aisa loudly crying on the floor and kicked Gordon off the bed. Gordon went away.

Jessie tried to read, but the text in books were still distorted, and she couldn't be distracted by anything, not even her daughter. They left Jessie alone as they could most of the time, and she would search for the videos he posted on YouTube. She wanted to know more about him.

That was an old performance work. In the gallery, James wore a cactus bra and provoked a woman by gazing and approaching her face for trying to kiss her. After whispering her a few words, the female audience spat red juice in his face and poured it all onto his body. He got enraged, went away from the crowds who watched the performance and came back:

"Why did you do this shit to me? It was for one night!" he said. "It was one fucking night!" yelled James at the woman.

Another performance called "Bloodline" was dated two years ago but only posted a few days ago—on the stage, a black-capped man wore a *Scream* mask, and a conjurer dressed in white and wearing a tall bush hat and a yellow pompom mask stood on the other side. James came to sit down with both fists placed on the table, and the masked man commenced tattooing on his clenched knuckles. He was calm at the beginning, but his face started grimacing with a few drops of sweat falling down from his greasy hair. James began to make the laughing sound as it was hard to be bitter if you started laughing. He got up and walked to the conjurer then slowly put his clenched knuckles on a white cloth on the table, and then stamped his two fists. Then he went back to the masked man and let him check the words then went back to the conjurer again and showed the red message to the audience:

SURVIVAL

He then put down the fabric and punched very hard onto it almost twenty times. He held it up again smeared and bloodstained.

Only the bloodline matters, is that it? Jessie thought.

In the other ritualistic performance, James was wrapped in serapes—a recurring cultural symbol in his work—with a raga-like melody, a kind of traditional Indian music mixed with electronic dance music obstinately played in the background, a coriander-caped performer wrapped serapes around James. After he was completely cocooned, James moved to cast off the blankets in a frantic dance with crazed movements until the fabrics were almost gone off his body.

Jessie had done enough investigation and got so stimulated that she started to create on the paper with a short poem she cut from a book:

The winds must come from somewhere when they blow,
There must be reasons why the leaves decay!
Time will say nothing, but I told you so,

After searching for the meaning of the error message that had appeared on Facebook, she realized that she had been blocked by James after the last message she sent him. But she still didn't give up trying to talk to him. She commented under one of James's videos. Things were getting worse now that she didn't hear his voice, but she couldn't help thinking about jumping from a window, and it was not about dying but just merely a yearning for the action.

She almost booked a plane ticket to see her parents but didn't get the doctor's permission. They had a long drawn-out meeting one day with the social worker and the doctor who asked her to write down her three priorities in life for now: First, get recovered soon so she can go back to see her parents. Second, her nineteen-month-year-old daughter, and the last, to be a successful fashion designer so she could transfer all of her mandalas onto garments. These goals became a commitment and a "social contract" with the doctor and the social worker.

Gordon brought Jessie somewhere, but she was still flattened, not only from her medication but also about her sleepless nights. She didn't think the oral drugs worked at all, only the injection she got at the hospital. But she hated being shot by the needle deeply.

"Do you still love me?" asked Jessie in the car on the way home.

"I love you very much," he said. "Deeply." He never talked like this.

"Why? What made you love me?" asked Jessie.

"I love your everything—your smile, your voice, the way you talk, the things you do, I love all of you. I never said it to you, but I do love you very much," confessed Gordon.

She suddenly didn't know how she could leave this man now. Perhaps she was just a hopelessly incurable romantic, and she desired it more than any other woman. At night, she had some fleeting moments of sleep, but the tightness on top of her brain kept awakening her.

Her waking consciousness ran so well it lifted off the top area of the brain whenever she almost entered the sleep mode. She tried really hard to get her consciousness down into a state of inactivity—closing her eyes, lying still as though pretending to sleep. The stress of taking sleeping pills before bed every night made her feel more frustrated. She hated her awareness during the night. It was like putting her head underwater; the alertness was more precise than in the air.

She got off the bed, leaving Aisa and Gordon in a deep sleep (and snoring) and went to the next room, which was empty. She imagined walking in a circle in this room on the bed, but once she began her steps, she failed. The strolling exercise in the hospital didn't work here. It couldn't mediate her boredom and loneliness. The small dark room was gloomy and scary for any other thought. She went to shake awake Gordon and asked him to sleep with her in another room which had a small balcony.

It was two thirty in the morning, and Jessie's mind was still visible when Gordon fell asleep again beside her. She watched the black fence outside through the window.

Jump!

It was the voice from the bottom of her heart—clear and committed. She couldn't handle this anymore, so she went downstairs and took out the card that the nurse gave to her, a 24-hour lifesaving phone number. She called it, but nobody answered. Gordon went downstairs to check her.

"I have to go back to the hospital," said Jessie with a calm voice.

"Why?" he said. "What's wrong?"

"I want to die," she said feeling helpless.

"Okay. I will drive you," said Gordon and went to wake up his mom.

At his knock, his mom opened the door.

"We are going to the hospital," Gordon said. "Aisa is still sleeping by herself."

"What was wrong?" asked their mom, and without hearing what Gordon said, their mom understood. Jessie gazed the white light to the upstairs before closing the door.

The dashboard clock in the car read 3:15 a.m. They were on their way to the emergency department, just like driving in a light carriage on a familiar road. Jessie waited for Gordon to pay for the parking, and they walked into the hospital together. They were sent to a room equipped with a bed, a desk, and a chair. Jessie started feeling anxious about staying here, and it seemed like she heard James's voice come back to talk to her, but she consciously rejected it and used her whole body to feel the weirdness as her upper part, and lower part of the body could be separated.

The doctor came in after a long waiting time.

"What was wrong?" said the doctor sitting down and looked at Jessie.

"Someone tried to have sex with me just now! He was controlling my body. Look!" she said and looked down her lap.

Her limbs twitched slightly—nothing unusual. But she felt someone pulled her nerves playfully inside so that she danced like a marionette. She didn't want to hurt, slap, or hit any part of the body since the action would make her think of Meng. The doctor didn't say anything but wrote down the diagnosis and went away.

Gordon told her to cross her arms in front of her chest against the wall. He stood behind her and put his hands on her back. Jessie didn't ask Gordon his reason for doing so because she was extremely helpless and would take anyway to change the situation.

He told her to take a very deep breath. She did this twenty times and held onto the last breath. When Gordon felt she was motionless from the breath, he gave a very firm and intense pressure from her back.

"Ah!" she shouted. "What are you doing?"

That was a very sudden action—faster than what she could react to. She felt the tightness on top of her brain was almost blown up in an immediate moment.

"Try again. Don't overthink," he said.

She did the same posture again and concentrated on the exercise for another twenty breaths. Once again, she held the last breath and felt it settle in her chest… behind her eyes… in her brain…

Then, all of a sudden, Gordon was forcing her back. "Hey, hey, wake up!" he said. "Are you okay?"

Where am I? she asked herself. *What are these?*

She slowly opened her blurry eyes and saw the white wall, medical device, a narrowed examination bed. She felt like she had woken up from a deep sleep.

"What's happened? How long did I sleep?" she asked Gordon on the floor.

Jessie hadn't felt such a release for a long time. Now she felt comfortable. Calm. She had fainted for around fifteen seconds as Gordon said. Gordon held her onto the bed and left her staring at the ceiling. She grabbed her phone to look at her albums of photos. She tried to recollect what was going on in her life in each shot. While browsing the photo she saw tons of pictures of Aisa: climbing in the playground, eating in the restaurant, making a goofy face at home, standing posture at the zoo.

She cried. She missed her intensely.

The nurse came to get her and gave her a gown. Gordon went back and brought her belongings. While the nurse brought her back to the mental health unit, passing by the nursing station, she saw the seclusion room where she'd stayed before. She was assigned to a different ward, one that equipped two beds. Jessie lay on her sickbed—the other empty bed.

At dinnertime, she asked Gordon to bring the food she liked from outside. While strolling, she saw an old man who sat cross-legged with bare feet under the window in the TV hall. He bowed his head as though praying with the meal on the floor. Today seemed like his first day.

Chapter 9

Jessie the Galaxy

After dinnertime, the nurse carried in a needle kit and told Jessie to lie on the bed. She lowered her pants halfway to let the nurse give her an injection. That was a 12 mg risperidone shot to stabilize the dopamine synthesis capacity. Jessie did not reject any treatment; instead, she was very cooperative.

That afternoon in the TV hall, Jessie met the old man who'd seemed to be praying on the ground the other day. His looked like a mixture of Popeye and Ben Kingsley.

"Hi," he said and watched her sitting down.

"Hi," said Jessie, looking at his wrinkled face and shrivelled mouth without a tooth in it. "What's your name?"

"Dasa."

"What brought you here?" said Jessie.

"I got a heart attack from my ex-wife," said Dasa.

"Heart attack? How?" said Jessie.

"Oh, how! She is a witch. It's complicated to explain," said Dasa. "Look…"

He pulled his pants and exposed the glans of his penis.

"Do you like it?" he said.

It was a peach pink and erect without a foreskin.

"It's pretty," said Jessie.

"Do you want to suck it?" said Dasa.

Jessie didn't respond to him.

"Suck it," said Dasa.

She approached his cock a little bit and moved backwards. Looking at his cock, she thought about her ex-boyfriend. The colour, shape, and condition under the sunlight. She was amazed by this old man—he had to be in his seventies—to still have such young flesh. She thought of the same sitting position with her ex-boyfriend, and she helped with it.

"Do you still have a sex life?" asked Jessie.

"Yeah, when I go to massage, I'll fuck the girls. They are Asians, and they love it," said Dasa putting his cock back in. "I have enough money, you know. I don't need to work. I get five thousand bucks every month from the government."

Jessie talked a little bit about her family, and after a short moment of silence, Dasa spoke.

"What kind of car does your husband drive?" he asked.

"Audi."

"Oh, he is rich!" said Dasa. "Don't leave him."

"How did you divorce your ex-wife?" she said.

"Oh, that was a horrible story," he said. "She was a drug abuser. She took my money and ran away."

"Do you take drugs, too?" Jessie asked and watched him.

"No! I only take red pills for sleep," said Dasa. "It's similar to marijuana, but it makes you sleep well."

Jessie told him that she also had trouble sleeping, so Dasa wrote down the pill's name and the pharmacy on the paper.

"Not everyone can access it," said Dasa, "so give the pharmacist this note, and he will give you this pill."

"Okay."

"You won't be able to get it anywhere else," said Dasa.

The next morning, the nurse who helped with her injection called Jessie out to the balcony.

"Come, Jessie, I want to talk to you."

The nurse sat on the parterre on the balcony. "You are not allowed to spend time alone with men."

"Okay," said Jessie.

"Do you feel that you have to be intimate with every man?" asked the nurse chewing her gum.

After a short hesitation, Jessie answered. "No."

"Why did you come back here?" asked the nurse.

"I like it here," said Jessie. "I feel safe in here."

"I wouldn't want to stay here for any longer if I were you," said the nurse swinging her legs. "I feel exhausted staying here, and I come to do my job."

Jessie looked at her brown skin; she had a few pimples on her cheeks. A brilliant girl, when she talked, even with her mind constrained in the hospital. She freed her bun of curly hair and relaxed and stretched her arms. Jessie wished that one day she could be like her. She knew this time she was just coming back as a guest and an observer.

In the afternoon, Jessie passed by the ward and saw Meng sitting up in bed, crying. She didn't dare to comfort her. Brian and Karen were still in the hospital and spent the most time sleeping. Sometimes Jessie would ask Karen to play poker or draw mandalas with her. She liked to play bingo with the therapist and the in-patients as well. She loved the sound of the brass cage when it was rolling the balls, the light moving texture of the calling board. There was a snack as a reward from the therapist if you won the game.

Once Dasa stretched his leg to rub her leg under the table when they sat face-to-face, and Jessie instinctively pulled quickly away and even slouched down to take a look at his legs.

"I don't know why is that you made me horny when I saw you!" said Dasa helplessly when they sat together in the hall.

That day, someone asked Jessie something, but she didn't know how to respond. Dasa stretched his legs to rub Jessie, but she didn't pull her legs back and saw Dasa didn't look at her, but that was comforting in its own way.

During another therapy session in the meeting room, Eileen gave them some papers to write down some words about feelings.

"Anything!" said Eileen. "Anything that you can think of. Just write it down."

After a long pause grasping the pen, Dasa placed it down on the table. "I am totally blank right now. I don't know what to write."

"Any words, Dasa. Happy or angry or sad," said Eileen. "How do you feel right now?"

"I am happy when you say 'happy'; I am angry when you say 'angry.' I'm feeling what you are saying," said Dasa looking at the white paper. "I don't know what to write."

Jessie smiled and wrote 'grumpy.'

Later that day, strolling the hall, she made up her mind that she wouldn't come back anymore even though she felt it was like her second home. She went to check what Brian was doing—one last chance to talk to him. He crossed his legs asleep in his tiny single room. Brian has been sleeping for the whole day. Something was wrong with his brain, she'd heard he had a severe crash, a motorcycle accident.

A short bespectacled Caucasian man with a limp walked in with his cane. It was his first day. Jessie approached him with curiosity.

"Hi, I'm Jessie."

"Hi." he with a smile. "David."

He looked a little like a mix with Bill Gates and Woody Allen but much younger.

"What brought you here?" said Jessie walking with him around the hall.

"Oh! I'm not psycho," said David, hobbling. "I was transferred from the rehabilitation department. I'm just here for part of my treatment."

"What's happened to your legs?" said Jessie.

"I've gone through a series of big surgeries. I fell from the tenth floor when I went to check the construction site for my building and tripped on an exposed wire," said David. "Thank God that I am still alive!"

"Do you want to sit down and talk then?" said Jessie looking at his black cane.

"Oh, no! I'm fine. I need to exercise anyway."

"Are you a builder?" asked Jessie.

"No, I owned a paint shop. I'm too smart to finish my university and went into investments. I owned two apartments," said David proudly.

"Wow! You are a legend! Where's your paint shop?"

"It's in Tsawwassen," he said and sat on the chair in the hall after all.

After a while, David's dad came to visit him, so Jessie left him.

Gordon had brought her favourite chicken meal in. She was so happy about it, she ate it right away in the hall. Brian came with a drowsy look and looked at the lunch that she almost finished.

"Do you want some?" said Jessie watching Brian sat in the front.

Brian nodded, so Jessie pushed the rice box to him and gave him her chopsticks. He was so starving that he grabbed right away and gobbled it up.

It was time to get the injection.

The bi-weekly injection was too much for her now although, in the beginning, she felt the shot was a lifesaver. She lay face down on the bed and thought: *Is this how I'll be for the rest of my life?*

The time was getting slower, and she'd count how many hours had passed. She began to eat a snack to kill time—a pack of chips she won a Bingo last time—she'd ask Gordon to buy more for her.

"I never had the habit of eating chips," she told Dasa with her mouth full. "I don't know why I'm starting now."

"Because you are surviving," said Dasa.

She finally got a checkup with the doctor in the meeting room.

"Have you heard of any strange voice or seen strange things?" asked the young doctor.

"No."

"Have you had any thoughts to harm yourself or people?"

"No."

"Did you take medication on time?"

"Yes," said Jessie. "When can I leave here?"

"I'll discuss it with the other doctor," he said, capping his pen and closing his book. "It shouldn't be long."

Wasting time in the hospital now was boring. Jessie missed her daughter deeply. In the afternoon, she played poker with Karen, who told Jessie that the reason she came to the hospital was that her sister died in a car accident. But as soon as Jessie asked about a little detail of the crash, Karen held her hands up, sat bolt right up and then flew from the table like a wind, leaving Jessie sitting there with her cards.

I'm so close to winning! Jessie thought looking at Karen's cards.

Dal, the Indian client, came to visit her with his family—a son and a daughter. His wife brought a big bouquet following aside. Dal introduced his family to Jessie, who just woke up in the afternoon and smiled at them. His wife brought the children away and left Dal in the ward.

"How are you?" said Dal.

He would never know this talkative little woman could be in a psychiatric hospital.

"I'm okay," Jessie laughed.

"I'm sorry about missing your call that day," said Dal. "I was so drunk the night before."

Jessie shook her head and smiled. They wouldn't be getting in touch if there wasn't a business relationship between them. After a long pause, his wife came inside. It was the first time Jessie had met Dal's wife.

Dal was six foot one, a giraffe-tall brown man with thick black hair and shaggy eyebrows sternly blown off the hill, a hawk-bridged nose beneath the brow of a mountain, a perfect plaster model to draw. His wife wore a casual black sari. She had darker skin than Dal. With big eyes fluttering her long eyelashes as swiftly as butterfly's wings, she was cute as a doll and had known how to rise above her status as a pariah.

"Get well soon, okay?" said Dal as though he were taking to a younger sister.

Jessie waved to their children and watched them leave. She couldn't wait to go home, too.

"Get me out of here! You can't lock people like this. Not to anyone!" yelled Karen in front of the nursing station. "Buzz the door, my smoking time!"

"It's not your time yet!" shouted the nurse's cold voice.

Everyone got half an hour smoke time downstairs nearby Starbucks. Now Jessie realized Ikhlas had also been downstairs having a smoke. A new patient caught her attention because Melissa made good friends with Brian. This was a distinct combination of insanity. The first few days when Jessie came back to the ward. They were discussing wiretaps. Brian had the newspaper in hand and a pen hooked on his ear.

"That's very possible," said Melissa, "including the phone."

"We got to find a way to break the jail!" said Brian.

They stood in a small circle with the other man, who was also a new face for Jessie. When they were talking about injections and medication, Jessie jumped in.

"Hey, I got a shot just now!" she said proudly.

Their conversation stopped for a moment then recommenced.

"So what's your plan?" said Melissa.

"Keep calling," said Brian nipping the pen in his mouth.

"I'm in," said Melissa with a smile hovering on her lips.

"I'm in," said Jessie stepped forward into the circle although she wasn't quite sure what they were talking about.

Melissa wore a pair of big round brown plastic glasses. She had long wavy hair that caught the orange glow of sunset as it shined upon her pale speckled face and skinny body. She was an authentic hippie.

Melissa crossed her arms in front of her chest when she talked with Jessie on the balcony.

"How do you survive?" asked Jessie.

"Well, my parents support me, and I got a few allowances from the church."

"Can I get allowance even I am not a Christian?" asked Jessie since she was going to move out.

"I think it's for everyone. I just filled out the form and get approved by the staff."

"May I ask how much you got?"

"Not so much. It's five hundred bucks every month."

"That's quite an amount!" said Jessie.

"What do you depend on to live then?" asked Melissa.

"I want to write a book."

"That's an ambitious dream!" said Melissa watching Jessie's slight smile. "Great! Maybe one day I'll see your book on a rack in the bookstore."

The exercise became drawing mandalas in the hall.

"Can I have more colouring sheets, Susan?" asked Jessie to the occupational therapist who led the bingo game and was in charge of the daytime activities.

"There you go." Susan handed out some sheets to her.

No one would draw except for her.

"Not this," said Jessie. "Can I have the totem one? Do you have the raven?"

"Hold on. I might have some more in the storage room. Let me go check," said Susan walking into the storage room where they stored a bunch of board games, books, and DVDs.

The therapist finally got out a pile of colouring sheets for her, but the patterns were not what she wanted.

"I'm sorry, but I couldn't find any ravens. But I'll go print some out from the Internet later," said Susan, locking the door with one of the keys hang on her neck.

It doesn't matter anymore, thought Jessie colouring a butterfly.

"Little girl, you are still here!" The Chinese grandma was surprised to see her. "Don't come back anymore. You are too young to be here! You are wasting your time!"

Jessie gave her a smile and bowed to colour. Jessie asked the old grandma's phone number because she would like to visit her after, but the numbers and her name written on the note didn't look like a real one because of the deliberate stroke. Jessie might keep in touch with Karen as she asked her phone number as well. They could be good friends after.

"I can't stand it here any longer," Dasa said. "When can I get out of here?" He was wearing a thick grey hoodie (as a patient who would be discharged soon he got the privilege to wear the casual attire). "Get me fucking out of here! This is the worst place I have ever been." Dasa scowled and left after hearing the nurse's answer.

Jessie was envious of Dasa and his attire because she was still in the brown gown. He never talked to her ever since the warning of body contact. She tried to approach him, but she felt she had nothing to tell him. Keeping her distance from people made her think about going back to the normality—she was recovering.

"It is lucky to have you as a wife," said David sitting on the chair, watching Jessie stroll his way.

Jessie felt flattered by what he had said and gave him a big smile. *This is it.* There was no further discussion about this kind of topic since the boundary couldn't be any more explicit than this after marriage.

The next morning, Karen screamed and ran out of her room. She went to complain to the nurse that someone lay on her bed naked. Jessie went to check her room and found David on his back with his penis exposed and erect. No one knew his intention.

Jessie was discharged the next day.

Afterword

I left Jessie behind in the isolation room of the psychiatric unit in Richmond hospital in 2014. Driving by the hospital, there was a feeling of the déjà vu that faded away only slowly over time. The mental illness—a doctor's diagnosis of paranoid schizophrenia—was like a bloody truth.

The isolation room (also called the seclusion room) for psychosis worked. The intensive care and psychiatric unit worked. The injections worked, and the occupational therapy worked. Besides the biweekly injections of Risperdal Consta, the oral meds were forever being adjusted: escitalopram tablets 10 mg (an antidepressant given on May 26); lorazepam 1 mg (for short-term relief of the symptoms of excessive anxiety given on June 20); zopiclone 7.5 mg (which acts in the brain to aid sleep given throughout July and August)—all of these were somehow *not* working.

My body function had crashed. My menses were gone, which meant the regular physical cycle of a healthy woman was destroyed. It made mute protest against the intense treatment, which disturbed me more than mental illness because I thought of my daughter. I was fortunate to have her and my husband—who didn't regard my psychoneurosis with contempt. But I could neither convince nor prove to the psychiatrist yet that I could recover, in such a short period of time, from schizophrenia.

I was annoyed by the consultation with the mental health team every three weeks; I was monitored as to my daily intake of pills by taking them in the pharmacy at scheduled times; I doubted myself about the possibility of postnatal depression or a disorder from lactation. It was an unexpected journey—like sailing in the galaxy—and the breastfeeding was a milky way that was far beyond anything else.

One year later, I looked though recommend friends on Facebook and saw Ikhlas's profile. He died one year later after we met. I don't know how he died, but his death grieved me. I tried to contact Karen, but the phone numbers were not assigned. I bumped into the quiet Asian girl who worked as a clerk in an art store. Of course, she couldn't recognize me, so I didn't say anything, but I saw she wore a pair of thick clear plastic spectacles. She was just another ordinary person who gave me a receipt and my change. Ultimately, I didn't have a single wardmate to contact.

It had been six years when I searched James again through Facebook using a different account—because he blocked me—he has his own child and happily lives with his artist wife. The artwork he made became more refined and thoughtful than before, but it couldn't attract and distract me from life anymore.

"Mommy, do you love me more or Daddy?" Aisa sat behind on the passenger seat.

"I love you, baby," I said while driving the car.

I love my life, love my family, and enjoy my job and living conditions at present. I told Gordon that I didn't want to split after the second discharge. He'd already applied and filed everything, and because we slept separately, it would have provided solid basis for divorce by law—all I needed to do was sign the papers. But I didn't.

Our marriage and sexual relationship have improved over the past few years, and we still enjoy a strong partnership. Once the marriage was determined and committed—change became the key to open happiness. Nothing is more essential and more fulfilling than making the one you love content. Everyone shapes their own life.

One time, after picking up a vest for Aisa, we were in a check-out line at the department store and the clerk the was serving Gordon.

"I like your tattoo!" she said looking at his hand—a tattoo on his ring finger with a JG pattern on top.

"Did it really hurt?"

Gordon nodded his head and smiled.

After ringing us through, the clerk walked out from behind the till and intentionally gave the bag to me. I think she wanted to know what his wife looked like.

I gave her a smile back.

"Thank you."

I appreciated that she was the first one to notice Gordon's ring tattoo, and she reminded me of what marriage is. The question she asked was meaningful and metaphorical for us.

I have had another episode after writing this book. It was triggered by another man, an actual man that arrived in my life. We only see each other once a year, however I got admitted in the hospital afterwards. I am certain this time, that I have paranoid schiqophrenia, but the discharge doctor note indicate that I have "unspecified psychiatric disorder."

www.ingramcontent.com/pod-product-compliance
Lightning Source LLC
LaVergne TN
LVHW041645060526
838200LV00040B/1728